BEFORE AND AFTER NORTH DORGENOIS: GROWING UP IN THE SIXTH WARD

by Ebony Bolding

Neighborhood Story Project
Red Rattle Books/Soft Skull Press
New Orleans, Louisiana
Brooklyn New York
2005

Other books from the Neighborhood Story Project

Between Piety and Desire by Arlet and Sam Wylie
The Combination by Ashley Nelson
Palmyra Street by Jana Dennis
What Would the World be Without Women? by Waukesha Jackson

Series Editor: Rachel Breunlin
Graphic Designer: Gareth Breunlin

Before and After North Dorgenois
ISBN 1-933368-31-4
ISBN-13 978-1933-36831-3

© 2005 by the Neighborhood Story Project

Let us hear from you. www.neighborhoodstoryproject.org.
Neighborhood Story Project
P.O. Box 19742
New Orleans, LA 70179

Soft Skull Press, Inc.
55 Washington St, Suite 804
Brooklyn NY 11201
www.softskull.com

Distributed by Publishers Group West
www.pgw.com

Text pages produced on 70 lb. Lynx Opaque, Smooth Finish,
donated by Weyerhaeuser Company, Fort Mill, South Carolina
Tango Coated Cover, donated by MeadWestvaco, Stamford,
Connecticut, manufactured in Covington, Virginia
Printing and binding donated by WORZALLA, Stevens Point,
Wisconsin USA

DEDICATION

THIS BOOK IS DEDICATED TO MY FAMILY AND THE PEOPLE WHO
LIVE IN THE SIXTH WARD.

ACKNOWLEDGEMENTS

Thanks to my mother for giving birth to me, making this possible and for telling me I can do it. To my daddy for just being my daddy and being there for me.

Thanks to my teachers, Abram and Rachel, for pushing me everyday, making me a better writer and putting up with my not so good days. Thanks to Rachel for editing interviews and Abram for helping me take photographs.

Thanks to Tammi for being so interested in my project and for participating in my book committee.

Thanks to the whole NSP: Kesha, Jana, Ashley, Ceirod, Sam and Arlet for making boring days fun.

Thanks to Lauren for taking time to type up my work.

Thanks to Ms. Boswell for giving me the opportunity to interview, and also for the Jamaican food, cause it was good.

Thanks to Mr. Tim the builder– keep up the good work.

Thanks to my neighbors, Ms. Thelma, Mrs. Ivory, and Mr. and Mrs. Schneider, Ms. Ewell, and Corey for letting me interview them.

Thanks to Davey for giving me a good laugh.

Thanks to my brother Brandon for just being aggravating and stupid.

Thanks to my brother Nakia for believing in me.

Thanks to the haters for hating and thinking this wasn't possible.

And last, but not least, to the Bayou Road Boys: Mike, Roy, Crisshawn, and, of course, my brother Brandon again.

Thanks to all of you who had anything to do with my book.

TABLE OF CONTENTS

GROWING UP IN THE SIXTH WARD

The wards in New Orleans are from voting districts. They were made at a time when most black people couldn't vote. Nowadays though, people my age represent their wards as if where you're from on the ward map says everything about you. They do have some people who are deuce ward; they don't really know where they're from. One day they're from here and the next they're from somewhere else. Some people will say they're from a certain ward just to try and be down with the crowd. I've never had that problem cause for as long as I can remember, I've been staying in the Sixth ward.

Some people say the Sixth Ward is small, but it's big enough for me. Esplanade Avenue is the downtown boundary of the neighborhood. It divides the Sixth and Seventh Wards. The Avenue has a neutral ground with lots of big trees. On both sides of the stree it has beautiful up and downstairs historical houses. Esplanade isn't a street where people hang out. People just walk their dogs and catch the Esplanade bus.

The Sixth Ward ends on Lafitte Street, which borders the Lafitte Public Housing Development. Sometimes I'll walk over to Lafitte to get a frozen cup. It's really different than the other end by Esplanade. People spend a lot of time outside and there's always something going on. Broad Street is the boundary between the Sixth and Fifth Wards. Broad is mainly businesses, including corner stores, barber shops, nail shops, fast food places, with a few houses in between. On Broad you can find the Zulu Social Aid and Pleasure Club, which hosts lots of parties and events. Come Mardi Gras time, Zulu parades through the Sixth Ward on Orleans Avenue. On Broad, you can also find Orchid Seafood where my mom and I like to get shrimp and oyster sandwiches.

The last and final boundary to the neighborhood is Rampart Street, which divides the Sixth Ward from the French Quarter. The houses around Rampart in a part of the Sixth Ward called Tremé are being fixed up and new people are moving in, just like around the blocks near Esplanade.

I like the middle of the Sixth Ward. There's always something to do. The houses are really old and they need lots of work. But to me, it's not the houses that make up a neighborhood, it's the people. I like to see my neighbors come outside and enjoy themselves. You only have one life to live. And on Sundays, the streets get taken over with people as second lines parade through the streets. We have some of the best second lines in the city. Yup, they surely do be rollin. They have people from all different wards coming to see them.

When someone asks me where I'm from, I'm proud to say the Sixth Ward. As I was coming up, people used to tell me, "Never forget where you come from." My brother and his friends talk about the Sixth Ward all the time. They rep their ward hard everywhere they go—they ain't never scared. Some people think the wards are stupid, but to me it makes sense because usually you grew up around your ward. Some people get beef out of it, which doesn't make sense to me.

When I was around ten years old, my family moved to edge of the neighborhood a block and a half away from Esplanade on North Dorgenois. It felt like a ghost town compared to the streets I grew up on. Although it is still within the boundaries of the Sixth Ward, sometimes I didn't feel like I was still a part of the neighborhood.

In this book, I am going to explore my experiences in the Sixth Ward. I am going to tell you about my relationship with my family and talk about the different ways people in the Sixth Ward think about the neighborhood. Some people don't associate with it at all and other people fight for it and end up suffering the consequences.

Sometimes where I live is called dangerous. In this book, I've asked my family, friends, and neighbors if they think that's true and whether the police are helping the situation. One thing that I've learned from writing this book is that there are all sorts of ways people look at my part of town.

PART I: MY FAMILY

My family is my mom, dad, and two brothers Nakia and Brandon. As a kid, I just had one parent in the household. My parents split up when I was three. But you know, I was young. I really didn't know any better. My parents are still the best of friends. October 25, 2004 made twenty-five years of marriage. My daddy always calls my mama and tells her happy anniversary. I always think about if my daddy lived with my mama, brother, and me. I think it would be nice. When we were living on North Johnson Street, my daddy used to come over and drink beer with my mama's boyfriend. He had better gotten cool with my daddy because he was going to be around no matter what.

People used to say Nakia and Brandon looked like my daddy and I looked like my mama, but I say I look like myself. My mama always say, "You gotta look like somebody." Sometimes I wish I was the oldest so I could boss my two brothers around, but I like being mama and daddy's baby girl, too. I like that it's just one of me and two knucklehead boys. Brandon used to try to get his way, but I told him, "I'm the baby. I'm supposed to get my way." When we were little, we went to Craig Elementary School. We walked to school together every morning with my mother because she worked in the cafeteria. After school and on Saturday mornings we watched cartoons together, but now he doesn't have much time to hang out with me because he works and then goes clubbing on the weekends.

As we moved from neighborhood to neighborhood, we always got along with the neighbors pretty well. My mama would sit on the porch with Ms. Gene and talk about the other neighbors and how their children are growing up so fast while I played outside with my best friend Trinice. She lived around the corner from my house on North Johnson. We went by each other's houses and played with our baby dolls, rode our bikes and sometimes played house. Trinice's brother Brian was ill and also mentally retarded. He was a sweet young man, but needed help with everything. He couldn't walk, talk or eat by

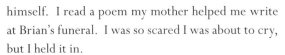

himself. I read a poem my mother helped me write at Brian's funeral. I was so scared I was about to cry, but I held it in.

I think one of my biggest struggles is my shyness. My elementary teachers always labeled me a shy, quiet, sweet little girl. I don't know where I get it from because my mother's not that way at all. Most of the time it happens when I have to introduce myself to people or I'm around a lot of unfamiliar people. In high school, I kind of went out of it because one of my teachers told me if I read in class I would get extra points. Really, the real reason why I started reading was to show the students that I could read, too.

When I was in dance class, my teacher taught me how not to be shy. She told me when I'm performing at my recital just look at one of my family members the whole while I'm on stage. I was looking at my mama. Most likely if I paid attention to everyone in the audience I would have messed up. I didn't want

to make myself look crazy in front of everyone in the audience.

When I started to write this book, once again I began by looking at my family. We've always been close. They've come to dance recitals, graduations, and parades that I've marched in, and so when I told them I was writing a book they were excited. My mother told me to stick with it and don't start and not finish. I wrote about my family members, did interviews with them, looked through old family photo albums to find pictures of us when we were young, and took other photographs. I also interviewed and photographed my brother's friends, the Bayou Road Boys. I asked everyone what they thought of the Sixth Ward and everybody had their own opinion. I wasn't shy at all because they weren't strangers to me. I grew up with them.

NAKIA AND TAMMI

Ring, ring. I answer the telephone and the person on the other line says, "Hello, may I speak to Mrs. Henrietta Bolding?" Guess who that was? My oldest brother Nakia playing on the phone again. He thinks that I don't know it's him pretending to be someone else.

Nakia is twelve years older than me. We didn't always get along. When I was little, he used to holla or laugh at me. By my being younger and having soft feelings, it used to make me cry. When I was younger, I used to believe him when he'd tell me, "You was adopted. Mama found you." Now, I just say, "No, Brandon is adopted. Mama found him." He thinks it's funny to call me Big Head when he's the one with the big head.

When Nakia was going to Bell Junior High, he met Tammi Cunningham and they became boyfriend and girlfriend. Tammi was raised in the Sixth Ward in a house down from Craig with two brothers and two sisters She went to elementary school there, too.

I don't remember being introduced to Tammi. I just always remember her being in my life. She's like a real big sister to me. I can tell her a lot of stuff. I used to go everywhere with her when I was younger. We have the same taste and style. When Tammi and I go to the mall, she gets my OK before she buys something and it's the same way with me. Tammi gets her lil' joke on, too. She calls my family the Big Head Family. What she don't know is that when she has a baby with Nakia their baby's head is going to be huge since they both have big heads.

Nakia moved into Tammi's house on St. Philip Street while they were still at Bell. My mama said, "I guess he thought he was grown. He fell in love and wanted to be with her. I didn't want him to leave, but he did fine." Nakia and Tammi have been living together ever since, but they were never very far away. I slept over by Tammi's house on St. Philip Street every other weekend and when they moved next door to us on North Johnson, I was over at their house everyday. I couldn't imagine Nakia without Tammi or Tammi without Nakia.

MOVING TO N. DORGENOIS

I was very upset when my mama told Brandon and me that we were moving from North Johnson Street. to our cousin's old house. They were buying a house across the river. and my cousin gave a good word to the landlord about my mother and that's how we got the house at 1234 N. Dorgenois between Barracks and Governor Nicholls. My brother and I were getting older and we needed our own space. I was going to have my own room and you know what that meant—privacy.

On our side of the street, there are three houses along with a church and a hall. I live in a three bedroom, two-bath green and white upstairs and downstairs house. My mother's room is downstairs and so is one of the bathrooms. Upstairs is my and my brother's room and the other bathroom, My house is nice and cozy. The only thing I don't like is the high ceiling. It makes it hard to keep the house warm. I would rather have low ceilings and a brick house—they always seem warmer in the winter and cooler in the summer.

The trees are beautiful in their own way. If you look and stare at the trees you probably would see a shape or object. They are good for shade in the summertime, but they are also the reason it's so dark at night.

If it were up to me, there would not be an oak tree in front of my door. Other people say the oak trees are so beautiful but they don't have to be the one to clean up after them. I look at the oak trees as lots of work sweeping up leaves, pollen, and stinging caterpillars. We have something to sweep every season. When we have a hurricane warning, I worry that the trees are going to fall on our house.

My mom loves a clean house. She can't stand for Brandon and me to be all dirty. I help out by cooking. Brandon never helps cook but he always wants to eat. Nakia is a good cook. I guess he gets it from our mama. He'll always cook when I go to visit him. When people come by my house, I want them to feel like they're at home. Everyone likes to come and visit my house for the holidays because it's nice and roomy.

My house is a boring place to be. When I go outside it still be boring because there's nothing to do out there, either. Sometimes my mama will do my little cousin T'keyana's or my hair. Sometimes I play the video game Madden 2004 with Brandon. I always lose, but it's still fun. I just can't get the hang of it. At times it's fun when my mama, daddy and I just sit around and watch movies all day and eat popcorn.

When I get older I don't want a house like the one I live in now. I want a beautiful apartment with a fireplace in the living room, two bedrooms, two baths and a big yellow and white kitchen.

MY RELATIONSHIP WITH MY MOTHER

My mother's name is Henrietta but everybody calls her Mrs. Bolding. My mother is pretty short, petite and wears red lipstick that's striking against her black hair. She likes to come home from a hard day of work and sit down and watch TV. On Sundays she likes to lay in her bed and watch Lifetime or smoke cigarettes and drink a little beer with the lady around the corner. She's very creative. She knows how to sew, draw, and does a little bit of hair, too.

My relationship with my mother is not like most mothers and daughters. I do everything with her—cook, shop and watch tv. All that good stuff. Most teenagers are not as close to their mother as I am. At times I say stuff that I don't mean in my head when she is fussing, but half of the time it's because I can't handle it or sometimes I'm just tired of hearing the same thing over and over. Every day I hear the same old stuff, "You too young to be so tired. Clean your room Ebony."

I don't even much trip, because if she doesn't tell me, who will? She's just playing her part as a mother who cares. Sometimes I think she is being too hard on me but then I stop and think, "Well, maybe she just trying to make me strong." She always says, "Hurry up and get out of high school so you can go to college and become that nurse you want to be, then you can take care of me."

My mama is outspoken and independent—what she has, she worked for it. She's not dependent on anybody. I admire my mother for being outspoken; she won't let people talk to her crazy. My mother always says what she had to say—she don't cut corners. It's important because sometimes people will take your kindness for your weakness. I'm much more shy than her. It's something that I got on my own and I'll probably have for the rest of my life, but I think I'll have some of my mother's other ways.

My mama comes from a family of eight–three sisters and four brothers–and has always worked hard. She was born in Kentwood and moved to the city as a teenager. One time we drove to the country to see where she grew up. There was so much space some of the houses are more than a mile apart. She wanted to show me where her house was, but someone had torn it down.

She shares her life stories with me all the time. She is the baby of the family, too. She always tells me when she was a little girl her older brothers and sisters had to go in the field and pick apples and cotton. My mama was too young to go in the field, so she just sat down and watched. When she was old enough to go to school, she would catch the school bus with her big brothers and sisters. After school when they got off they used to race home to get the biggest plate for dinner. My grandmother would have their plates waiting on the table. I wish I had it like that when I come home and say, "I'm hungry," my mama says, "Girl, you old enough to fix yourself something to eat."

My mama always tells me, "You better watch me and learn something." That's how she learned how to cook. She'll say, "You not gonna get no husband like that, because all you like to cook is pasta, fried chicken, macaroni and cheese, and fried pork chops." I like other food but they take too long like gumbo and red beans. That's why I love fast food—mainly McDonald's. My mama says, "Girl, you gonna turn into a McDonald's." She doesn't like fast food that much. When she doesn't cook, she will order a shrimp sandwich or a Whopper combo from Burger King.

I always ask my mama about my grandmother who died when I was three. I ask her what was she like and how does it feel to not have her around anymore. She'll say, "Well, my mother was a sweet lady, and knew how to cook good. I wish she could still be here so she could see how big you, Brandon, and Nakia have gotten." As I get older my mama says, "I wish mother could be here and see how beautiful you are growing up to be."

INTERVIEW WITH HENRIETTA BOLDING

THE COUNTRY

Ebony: Where did you grow up?

Henrietta: I grew up in Kentwood, Louisiana.

E: How does Kentwood look?

H: It's just a small country town. Not too big. Not very many red lights. Maybe a high school and an elementary crossed with a middle school together. I can't even remember if it has a shopping center. But the country was great. I don't regret nothing about the country from when I grew up.

E: What was your mama like?

H: [My mama] was a country woman. She was a hard-working little woman. She did babysitting, she did housework, even field work. Whatever she needed to do to take care of us, she did it. My dad died when I was real young. It was eight of us, and I'm the baby. She couldn't afford to give us what we wanted– she gave us what we needed. She wasn't a huggin mom. But we knew that she was a loving person. She just took care of us [and] used to watch other people's kids, too.

We were brought up in church. I don't really think my mother was that religious, but she made us go to church every night! The church was in the neighbor-hood. It was a Sanctified church, and all them old people used to get the Holy Ghost. They used to be shouting, falling all out and stuff. My brothers and sisters and me used to be laughing! We just used to be laughing and laughing and laughing. I didn't know no better at the time, but I knew better after I got older. Now, I barely go. When I feel blessed, I go to church. I told you you're gonna have to start going, too. If you blessed, you got to show Jesus you appreciate him blessing you.

All I can tell ya is I don't regret my mama raising me. She brought us up very, very well. And I guess that's why I try to bring them up like that. Because she had good kids. Good kids. None of us are in jail, or prostituting, or on drugs. We just grew up to be good people.

THE CITY

E: What made you decide to move to New Orleans?

H: I moved to New Orleans when I was fourteen years old. My older sister Christine was living in New Orleans [and] we used to come down here in the summer with her. Eventually, my mom let us move down here when I was a teenager. Pretty soon after that, my mom moved down here, too. So we've been living here for—Oh, Lord— years and years.

My sister lives [on Dumaine], my other sister lives on St. Anthony Street. I got another brother that lives on St. Anthony, and I got a brother that lives around there on North Tonti. My mother was here, too. The only sister and brothers that I don't have here is a sister in Houston, Texas, my brother in Kentwood, and one of my brothers passed away.

We [rarely] go up [to Tangipahoa]. There's [barely any] body left. Besides my older brother, maybe some nieces and nephews, and a few cousins and stuff. [On my mom's side] I have one auntie out of twelve that's still living. Some of the people I went to school with look real, real bad, and if I see them I can't recognize them. A lot of them are dead.

Matter of fact, I went up there Saturday night. I didn't go to Kentwood but I went to Tangipahoa. My cousin had a birthday party up there, so me, my sisters and my nieces and nephews went up there. It looked quite different—they're building up a lot. It looked real different.

E: Where did you move in the city?

H: We was living on Tulane Avenue. After I made eighteen, I had my own job and everything and I got my own apartment [with] a girlfriend of mine. After that, I met y'all's dad. He used to work around the corner from where I was working. I guess he liked me and we started dating.

A couple of years down the line, we made a baby. We got married on the 25th of October and Nakia was born on the 29th. We stayed together and stayed together until Ebony was three years old. Then I decided that I was gonna take my kids and I was gonna go because—I'm not even gonna say it. He was doing something that he wasn't supposed to do. I left, and I never went back. Although he changed, I never did. You can forgive em, but I don't know if you could trust them anymore.

We try to be the best of friends because he's a very good person. He was a good provider. Matter of fact, I didn't even have to work and I got what I wanted because he had a very good job. He's still a good person, but he just can't be a husband to me anymore.

E: What are the biggest differences between living in the country and the city?

H: Big difference. I mean, you feel safer in the country. I've always felt like when you born in the city, you born in the streets. Seriously. All you got to do is just step out there and get in trouble. When you in the country, these houses are not piled up on one another— you might have to go a mile before you see somebody else's house. You stay home; you wasn't in those streets.

And we're living in the city but it's not safe. A lot of people get killed in the country, too, but it ain't like it is here. Not at all. Every time my kids leave out this house I'm asking God to protect them, send em back home safe.

I'm glad I grew up in the country. I'm a country girl, but I know I'm so used to the city I don't think I'll ever go back to the country to live—where the jobs at?

LIVING IN THE SIXTH WARD

E: What do you think about the Sixth Ward?

H: I don't believe in all that ward stuff. I mean, these kids caught up in that, but I didn't even come up talking about no Sixth Ward and Seventh Ward. What difference does it make? I'm not into that. Even if I wasn't from the country, it wouldn't matter what ward I live in. I think it's a stupid thing.

E: What do you do for fun?

H: Nothing. I don't do anything for no fun. I don't know how to have no fun. I don't do nothing but go to work and stay home. I guess having fun is over for me. What you think I do for fun?

E: You go to the casino.

H: Now Ebony, when the last time I went? I went to the casino what? Over a year ago?

E: What have you been most happy about in your life so far?

H: My kids. Raising y'all. Do I have to add more onto that? That's the best thing that came out of my life—having good kids that wasn't getting into trouble and being close with them and everything. And maybe my sisters and brothers. My life was happy when I first got married. Me and my husband used to do things together. But lately the best thing in my life is just having my kids in my life and raising them.

I don't know what I'm gonna do when they leave. I don't want to be on my own. I don't want to be without my kids. They can stay here forever as far as I'm concerned. I don't want to be left by myself. One of them already gone. Brandon, I don't know if he ever gonna leave. He don't want to spend his money on no bills, he want to spend his money on hisself. You'll probably be the same way, too. And fly away.

E: Has your relationship with your kids changed as we've grown up?

H: Yes indeed. It has changed a lot, Ebony. I do a lot of fussing around here because they room don't be clean and I don't like that. I find myself cleaning up behind y'all like y'all little bitty babies. I used to go in Brandon's room and there wouldn't nothing be on the hanger in the closet. Everything would be on the floor. I used to pick the stuff up, put it on hangers. How long did it last? No time.

When you get grown, you get responsibilities. You got to know what to do and how to do it. Y'all ought to be experts at cleaning up and doing this and that, being around my mouth fussing all the time. But, there's a lot of other things that they could be doing, in the streets—running the streets, getting in trouble. So, don't get me wrong: I mean y'all need to do what I tell you to do and do it right. Don't think I'm making excuses for y'all. No. I ain't.

E: If you had some things to do over again, what would be different?

H: No. There's nothing in my life that I would change. Not at all. Even the marriage. I wouldn't have changed that because I had a good husband. A loving person until he made those mistakes.

MY DADDY

My daddy's name is Issac Bolding. He was born in New Orleans and has been living in the city ever since. He has five brothers and four sisters. His mother died when he was a little boy. His father is still living; he is eighty-four years old. My daddy is average height, dark brown skin, has a beard, and always wears a hat. He used to be skinny; now he's a little fat. He looks like his father like my brothers look like our daddy when he was younger. My mama has two pictures—one looks like Brandon and the other one looks like Nakia.

My daddy works for the city and rides his bike to work and back. He rides around in a big orange truck mainly fixing the streets and unstopping drains. On the weekends, he likes to drink beer with his brother over on Dumaine Street in the Fifth Ward.

My daddy lives with his girlfriend but always comes to visit my brother and me at our house. He might not have been living in the same house, but he didn't ever forget his kids. He calls me Elmo, I guess, because of my squeaky voice. He's kind-hearted. If he has it, he'll give it to you. My mama gets jealous when he goes all out of the way for me. When my brother or somebody hits me he always says, "Don't hit my baby." The only time I get mad at him is when I have to split the money he gives me with Brandon. I tell him I shouldn't have to give Brandon any money because he has a job.

I remember when I was sick my daddy came and made me pork chops and red gravy over rice. My daddy is there for me most of the time. If he's not, I don't sweat it because some fathers don't have anything to do with their kids. I think he's doing his part being a father to his children. It takes a real man to take that big responsibility. I always joke with my daddy when he comes to visit. I say, "What time it is? You know Nina don't play that with you." He says, "I'm spending time with my kids."

Every time one of my friends come over I introduce him to them, they say he seems like he's nice. I say, "Yeah, he cool people."

INTERVIEW WITH ISSAC BODLING

Ebony: Where did you grow up?

Issac: We lived Uptown on First and Willard near Claiborne Avenue in a house full of kids—five boys and five girls.

E: What did your parents do for work?

My mother was a housewife [and] my daddy was a cement finisher. He just retired from that—he's been there for forty-five years.

E: How did you meet my mom?

I: I met her in a restaurant. I was working round the corner. I went there for some lunch and I saw your mother. I start talking to her, start dating, and got married.

E: How has your relationship with her changed over time?

I: We got a good relationship. We're friends. You know, just like sisters and brothers right now.

Henrietta: Say more.

I: Okay.

A: What kind of work do you do?

I: I work in Public Works on the vacuum truck – clean drains out. I've been there twenty-one years. [It's] just me and the driver, two to a truck—nobody bothering us or nothing. [We] get a lot of good talk from the public. When we go out there, they say, "Oooh, I'm glad to see you all out here."

A lot of people got a habit of putting stuff like oil down in the drain. It clogs it up; makes it harder for us to do our job. And then they blow grass and stuff in there. They figure that wouldn't do no harm—but it do a lot of harm! It gets mix in with that trash and stuff; it can be like plaster.

H: You got him talking now!

E: What is your relationship like with your kids?

I: Good. Nakia and I sit by my father's [in the] evening times and drink a few little beers. Some weekends [we'll] go fishing cross the river. We try to catch crabs out on the lake. You know, off the steps.

E: Has your relationship with us changed as we've grown up?

I: No. [You're] fine kids; don't give your momma no kind of problems or nothing. That's good.

E: What do you think about wards? Like, Sixth Ward, Seventh Ward...

I: Well, it don't mean nothing. I don't like what's happening. There's problems. Kids see one kid not from their ward, and they might fight or something, you know. Somebody's gonna get hurt. I don't like the wards. It's no good.

E: Did people talk about wards when you were coming up?

I: No. We didn't have those, like, First Ward, Second Ward. Ain't never heard nothing like that. 'til the eighties. [When I was comin up], they ain't had all that stuff goin on now in school—shooting, fighting, the gangs, and stuff. I tell my kids that all the time. We had none of that, you know.

Abram: A part of Ebony's book is a little bit about the shooting at John Mac. What do you think about all that?

I: I knew the little fella, too. I knew the little boy since his mama was carrying him in her stomach. I knew his brothers, his daddy—all of them. That was ridiculous the way they shot that little kid up in there like that.

(Telephone rings)

I: [Ebony] comes home from school [and] she got to check the messages. "Mom, any phone calls?" She's the one that check it, you know. (Laughs). Yep. When I was coming up, I didn't talk on the phone.

E: Excuse me?

I: You couldn't last a day without a phone in this house. She'll go crazy. (Laughs). [But she's] a good child. Sweet. Don't give her mother a bit of problems. Not a bit of problems. Her mother tell her to do something, don't get no backmouth or nothing. Just go and do it. Might be a little attitude, but she's gonna do it. (laughs)

E: Where did you learn to cook?

I: Coming up with three sisters older than me, I watched them in the kitchen. My mother had died, you know, [when] I was nine years old. They got older and I showed them a lot by cooking fried chicken, smothered chicken, a good pot roast. Potato salad goes along with that, some peas—that's a good Sunday meal there. [I] even showed Ebony a little bit. "Dad, this ready?" I said, "Ebony, get you a good dark brown, stick your fork down in there. You don't see no blood or nothing, it's ready to go."

E: What do you like to do on your free time?

I: Free time? I be at the house watching old John

Wayne westerns on television. Me and my friends go fishing. [We] get our little beers, get our little meat and bread. Half the time you be sitting, eating, drinking, and they be doing the fishing. I ain't really no fisherman, but I like it for the sport.

E: What are some of your favorite memories of our family?

I: Mmmm....well, coming around, you know, reminds me of when I was here with y'all. Like I said, you know, we're still close.

E: What have you been most happy about in your life so far?

I: Well, coming around on the weekends, spending time with my kids.

E: If you had to do some things over again, what would they be?

I: Try to get back with my family, and live in the house with y'all. You know. See you grow up. That would make me real happy.

NAKIA AND TAMMI'S WEDDING

November 20, 1999 is when my knucklehead brother Nakia got married to Tammi. The wedding was at St. Augustine Church in the Sixth Ward. Everybody and their mama was there. All my family on both my mom and dad's sides, people from out of town—even my sixth and fifth grade teachers from Craig because they were Tammi's teachers, too.

Brandon, my mama and daddy, and I were in the wedding. I was the junior bride and Brandon was the junior groom. The church was so big and beautiful. It was decorated with the colors from the wedding. I can remember it like it was yesterday. I have never seen anything like it. At most weddings you see one or two colors, but their wedding was a rainbow of green, pink, silver, blue, and burgundy. It might sound crazy, but if you were there, you would have liked it.

When we were by her mother's house, Tammi was so nervous getting dressed. She wanted everything to be straight. After we were dressed, I looked around and saw how beautiful everybody looked. On the way to the church, I rode with Tammi and the flower girls.

Before I walked into the church, I peeped in the church and saw all those people. I was nervous, but when I did walk in the church, all I could do was put a big smile on my face cause everyone was smil-

ing, too, and saying how beautiful I looked. After the maid of honor, bridesmaids, and flower girls, the bride finally came down the aisle. Her dress was sparkling. Everything was perfect. Nakia had tears rolling down his face when he walked to meet her half way.

The pastor was Father LeDoux and boy can he talk. The wedding was so long, people were getting restless and my feet were starting to hurt. I guess the pastor just got carried away. My cousin wrote a note saying that the limo people were ready to go. The wedding was finally over. Tammi and Nakia jumped the broom and everybody walked back down the aisle.

Nakia and Tammi rode together in a limo and I rode back with the bridesmaids. The reception took place at St. Luke's Hall on our block of North Dorgenois. Me, my hungry self is thinking, "Yeah, I'm bout to go get me something to eat," but the DJ said loud over the mic, "Would everybody from the wedding party please go to the front and take pictures?" I had forgotten all about pictures.

Man, the DJ was off the chain. He was playing rap, R&B, and old time music, you know, for the older people. Nakia and Tammi had their dance. Afterwards, Nakia and my mama had their mother and son dance to a Boys to Men song called, "Mama, You Know." The chorus goes, "Mama, you know I love you." Man, I danced the night away. Around this time, people were still doing the Bus Stop. Everybody was on the dance floor—old and young.

I always tell Tammi to save her wedding dress for me when I get married. I'm not planning on getting married anytime soon, but when I do, I will have a dress waiting for me.

Nakia and Tammi bought a brick home on the West Bank in Algiers. Tammi works at Vision Center of the South. Nakia does construction work for Kelbro. We don't see each other as much as we used to when they lived over here. Sometimes Tammi comes over on Fridays if she gets off of work early or she'll come over and eat lunch with my mom. Nakia still comes around every other day to get on my nerves and see what we're doing.

BRANDON

My brother Brandon is slim with light brown skin and waves. He is three years older than me. He's quiet at home but when he's around his friends he's not.

Brandon and I get along pretty well, but he gets away with a lot because he's not at home very much. My mama, brother, and I always talk about how Brandon is always touching and eating stuff that's not for him. He drinks my cold drinks that I keep in the refrigerator and eats my food.

He's aggravating in that way only older brothers can be. One night Brandon got on my nerves so much, I slammed his door and a picture fell off the wall. He says, "If you don't stop playing with me, I'm going to bat you in your mouth." He tells me, "I'm the big brother, you not my mama."

Brandon didn't finish school, but that doesn't make him less of a person. He's not out in the street robbing and killing people. He's just trying to work and make a lil' money. He works at Wendy's with his best friend Mike. They've known each other since Craig. Mike comes to get him almost every morning from home and brings him back. He's too lazy to go and get his driver's license. My mama used to let him drive her car. I wouldn't have let him drive nothing.

I get tired of hearing Brandon's mouth when he tells me I need a job. I say, "Just because you've been working at Wendy's all those years you think you can tell me I need a job. I'm going to get a job but just not yet." I get money from Brandon, but not enough. When he gets paid, he gives my mama some money and gives me some money some time. If I had a little brother or sister, I would buy them anything they wanted. I wouldn't be tight like Brandon.

We aren't close enough to tell him my problems. Brandon wouldn't know what to tell me. Plus, I wouldn't tell him anyway because I wouldn't feel right. He's a male and we don't have that kind of bond. We don't have a lot in common. I love to watch TV and really the only time he is in front of a TV is when he is playing Playstation 2 with his friends. Most of the time, he's out with his friends on Bayou Road in the Sixth Ward.

INTERVIEW WITH BRANDON

Ebony: What was it like growing up in our family?

Brandon: It was nice growing up with me, my mom and my brother and sister. I was always the quiet child. Everybody always looked at me different from everybody else cause I don't talk as much as everybody else.

E: How would you describe our relationship?

B: I say we have a good relationship. You get on my nerves a lot, but everything okay.

E: How would you describe our parents and their relationship?

B: Well, to say they separated, they get along well as friends.

E: What are some of your favorite family memories?

B: Going on the lake for like holidays and stuff. Going on family reunions. You see a lot of people you ain't seen in a long time. Eat. Have a lot of food. Music playing. We haven't had one of those in a long time.

E: Are you different around your family than you are around your friends?

B: No, I don't think so. I think I'm still the same person; the quiet one out of the whole group of my friends. Everybody say I'm the quiet one. Everybody be like, "Yeah, he be chilling. He quiet and everything."

E: What have you been most happy about in your life so far?

B: First thing, that I'm still living. And mother and father still with me. My little sister.

E: If you had to do something's over again what they be?

B: Yeah I wish the police wouldn't judge you by just looking at you thinking you drug dealers, just messing with you for nothing. I wish I could change that. It wouldn't have too many people getting killed. Shot up. Lot of people getting killed grew up with me. I went to school with them. Wish I could change all that.

Abram: Who are your heroes?

B: Mama

A: What about people you don't know?

B: Soulja Slim. He was a good rapper to me. Everything he rapped about was the truth. It was like, life.

E: How is North Dorgenois different from other parts of the neighborhood?

B: Dorgenois? It's a little quiet part of the Sixth Ward. It's not as rowdy as the rest. A lot of old people on the block.

E: How did you like it?

B:I liked it a lot—it was real nice, it was just that, it wasn't too many people outside walking around. I had to leave and like, come around Bayou Road to the little hangout to really have fun.

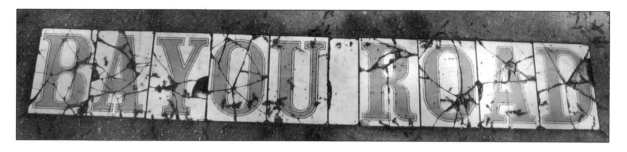

BAYOU ROAD BOYS

The Bayou Road Boys are a group of boys including my brother Brandon, Mike, Cody, Brice, Vernal, Head, Ray, Chrisshawn (aka Crazy), Glen and probably a couple more. They have known each other since they were young. They all grew up together and still hang out on Bayou Road, even though Head and Brice don't live there anymore. The boys enjoy standing outside talking and chillin. Clark Senior High is across the street, so you know they holla at some of the girls when they walk home. I consider them my big brothers because I have known them for so long. Brice calls Brandon Big Roach and me Lil Roach.

My favorite Bayou Road Boy to be around is still Mike. He's sweet and never mean to me. He never tells me no when I ask him to do something or when I ask him to bring me to Rite-Aid or Walgreen's. He's taken my friends and me to school and football games, too. Sometimes Brandon is the one who says no. He acts like he's jealous or something. One time when we had a half-day, Mike saw my friend and me walking from school. He stopped and loud-capped me in the middle of the street saying, "Why you not in school?" I couldn't do anything but laugh because I was so outdone.

When I say Bayou Road Boys you might think of a gang or something like that, but they aren't trouble-makers. Several times the BRBs have been harassed by them old stupid polices for nothing. You know, it's said, "You just get harassed and don't be even much doing nothing." Most police officers think every young black boy they see is up to no good, but that's a lie. They sometimes get low-down and dirty when they stop someone and run his name through the computer and can't find anything. They will put a quick charge on you—either crack or weed—and that's messed up, man! All the killers and rapists out here in this world and the police are out messing with young black boys.

When I was younger, I used to always ask Brandon to take me with him. Most of the time, he would say no, but sometimes he'd say, "Come on." I asked him if I could interview some of the BRBs for the book and he said, "Yeah." They're always representing their part of the Sixth Ward and now they'll be even more known.

Ebony: Describe the Sixth Ward for someone who has never been there.

Brandon: Sixth Ward a place where me and my other partners chill, we hang out; been hanging there for like, all my life. We used to have a little white abandoned house next to the apartments, but they tore our house down. It was like our little clubhouse. We used to hang out in there.

E: Why did they tear it down?

B: It was like, kinda, condemned. Yeah.

E: What do you like about the Sixth Ward?

B: I think it's a nice ward. [It's] really not too bad around this area right here.

E: When you think of the Sixth Ward, do you think of the people or do you think of the houses?

B: Yeah, the people—like the people that's out the same hood as me. Yeah.

E: How would you describe those people?

B: Most like family. Most of them I've been with ever since I was like four or five. Known em for like a good fourteen, fifteen years. And it's nice.

E: What would you change about it?

B: What would I change? Move a lot of girls in. Mostly boys stay around here and no girls.

E: How did ya'll become friends?

B: I knew him my first year at Craig. I knew him, but we wasn't as tight. But like in third grade, we became like best of friends. And ever since then we've been together.

E: What was Mike like as a little guy?

B: He was kinda fat—he was bigger than like what he is now. Not as tall or nothing, but he had more size on him.

E: Was [Brandon] quiet?

Mike: Yeah, he was a quiet one. I always get in trouble for what he's done.

Rachel: Are you more talkative around your friends than you are at home?

B: Yeah, cuz I have more to talk about. I've got more to talk about with my friends—I don't really know too much to talk about with other people.

Rachel: Do other people mean Ebony?

B: Like, I talk to her, but they say I'm quiet. But I feel nothing wrong with it. I feel that's how I been ever since I was a little boy, so I don't think that's gonna change.

E: If you had a day off work, what do you do?

B: Wake up, Mike come and get me, come around here, wait for everybody else to come, and that's most of what I do. On Sundays, we go out to Club Escape. That's on Claiborne—yeah.

E: What do y'all do together?

B: What do we do together?

M: We do everything together man! Except sleep and take a bath! (sirens) That's normal, see. Every day police come.

E: You get harassed by the police out here?

B: Oh yeah, a lot. A lot. For no reason, just for hangin out, chilling.

M: Just mindin our own business.

B: He's got Bayou Road on the back of his car. Yeah. And he got the Bayou Road gold chain—he representing with the necklace.

E: So why is it so important to represent this little part of the world?

B: Cuz Sixth Ward is like,

M: It's where we grew up at.

B: Yeah. We grew up around here. Most of the people we know—

M: Love this little area right here. It's all we got. If we had more, it'd be better, but this is what we gotta have right now. Sixth Ward is where all the second line bands and everything started, the Indians—that's where all that came from.

B: We got a lot of musicians.

M: And it's like we do whatever we can to survive in the Sixth Ward around here. There ain't much for us. We try with the band, make a little money –

E: What's the band that you were in?

M: I was in a band at school. At Clark, Bell, and Craig—

B: Yeah, Craig and Bell. Bell had the best junior high band in the city.

M: Like, everybody got their own way of getting their money—some people sell clothes, sell CDs, we got a lot of hustlas in the Sixth Ward—

B: Yeah, home of the hustla, yeah.

M: You catch a group of hustlas on every block. They got bad hustlas and good hustlas.

B: Anybody who's trying to get some money. Whatever it takes to get some money.

E: What's your definition of a bad hustla and a good hustla?

B: A good hustla is the legal way. A bad hustla is the illegal way. But sometimes you gotta take the bad way because people gonna put you in a predicament where that's all you can do, or you're gonna be in jail anyway, you know?

M: Some people have to stand out and sell drugs

B: Just to pay them.

M: Just to pay their money.

E: Why do they have to pay?

M: Because, like, say we standing right here—they'll take us to jail for "drunk in public" and we ain't got no say so or nothing.

B: There's no words. Once they put you in the car, you're gone.

M: Ain't nothing you can do about it.

B: And once you go to jail, you know, you have to pay court fees and everything—

M: In New Orleans, the judicial system is different. We guilty til proven innocent—other places its innocent til proven guilty. You see?

B: And we have the worst police—the crookedest police officers—the First District. Most corrupt district in New Orleans, and we got the most corrupt police force in the United States!

E: Here the police come.

M: See what I'm sayin? One time, one time me and him we got harassed on the corner—

B: Claiborne and Bayou Road.

M: It was cold – it was like, thirty-five degrees outside. They had us standing outside in our socks. Just standing there. No shoes or nothing on. We was just shaking.

The detective [took everything out] of the trunk [of my car] like we had done something. [He] draw the gun down on us for nothing. You know, about to go home and play a game. We had a Play Station and everything. And he see that, and still have us out there with our socks off in the freezing cold. Couldn't move. Somebody needs to do something about these police.

R: Tell me a little bit more about the First District. What makes them so corrupt?

B: They crooked. Like, they have their cell phones and they have their walkie talkies. See, if they arrive together they'll use their cell phone so they won't have to send it over the dispatch. They'll be harassing somebody and they'll call another car to help them out. You know, they can do anything. Put something on you, and after they put it on you then they'll call for the dispatch like they stopping you.

E: When you say the police come by, do they think

that you all are selling drugs back here, is that something that you deal with?

B: All the time. All the time.

M: If they pass right now they probably jump out right now. Just everyday. Knowing we ain't doing nothing here they'll come harass. If you get too smart with em, you're gonna roll out with em. You be like, "Why did you all come and do this to me?" They gonna be like, "Shut up." Like it's personal hate or something.

R: How do other people in the Sixth Ward see you all as a group? The Bayou Road Boys?

M: We don't have no beef within the ward. Everybody from the Sixth Ward, they try to stick together. We got love for everybody in the Sixth Ward— everybody that sends out love to us. [The Bayou Road Boys] are not a gang. It's just a group of people that have been together for a goodly while, and they stick together. There are other sets we hang out with like Gov. Nicholls and Roman, Dumaine and Miro. They have like St. Philip and Robinson, all these like sets in the Sixth Ward, like Bayou Road.

Crisshawn: Really, a lot of people think we're drug dealers, but we're not. When we were younger, we used to just hang out and play spades. It'd be twenty degrees, and we out here playing spades all day. As soon as we cut from school, or as soon as we cut from work, we come around here. But since we have gotten older, all of us work now, we don't really come around [as much].

RAY

E: What dreams do you all have for growing up?

R: Dreams? Everybody just hoping they get up on their feet; make some money and get up out tha hood. You gotta stay hood, but make some money, get a nice crib, nice girl, nice car. Be straight. That's all it's about That's the American Dream

Right now, I'm just chillin, you know. I'm a part time dishwasher.

E: Did you stay in school?

B: Nah. I was one of them bad kids; I went back and forth to jail.

E: Why were you going back and forth to jail?

B: Regular police stops, you know, tickets or something. Some petty stuff, you know. Same old thing everybody goin to jail for. It ain't about nothing to do with the Sixth Ward. You know, in the Ninth Ward, people doin the same thing.

BOYS

"Say girl. Say shorty," is what the boys say when I'm walking down the street. I get hollas from all types of boys. Fat, skinny, tall, short, fine, cute, ugly—they try to talk to me and most of the time I ignore them and pretend like they don't exist. One time a boy grabbed me by my arm and got mad when I told him not to touch me. He said, "But when I did that to that other girl she gave me her number." They be feelin played, but I don't trip because they be trying to get at me.

In general, the attention I get from boys don't mean nothing to me because all they gonna do is try and tell me stuff they think I want to hear. My oldest brother be saying, "You letting them lil boys buck your head up," because I stay in front of the mirror a lot. I tell him, "Nobody don't buck my head up because I know that I look good—I can see for myself."

A lot of boys are just about trying to impress their friends. Especially when a girl turns them down, they'll get mad and curse the girl out because he got played in front of his boys. I know this one boy who acts like he's two different people—when he's by himself he is good as gold but when he with his lil friends he want to be hard as a rock. He'll do stupid stuff, just to try and be down with his friends. Boys like to stunt too much like, "they got this," or "they

got that," but they know they don't have two nickels to rub together.

This one boy keeps trying to talk to me even though he was together with a friend of mine. When I asked him, "Didn't you used to mess with my friend?" He said, "So, but I like you now." I'm not even rockin like that. It would be so low down and dirty. I would never let a boy break up my friendship with my friends cause your friends will always be there when that boy has gone bout his business. All he gonna do is move on to the next girl.

PART II: HIGH SCHOOL

Brandon and I were living on North Dorgenois when we started high school. Even though we were just a block away from John McDonogh Senior High School, Brandon decided he wanted to go to Clark. For years, Clark was just a few blocks away on Esplanade, but the school board shut it down because someone set it on fire and it needed repairs. Brandon had to go to the new campus Uptown. When I started high school a few years later, I decided to go to Clark, too. I was so excited. I was going to be straight because with my brother and his friends around, no one was going to mess with me.

Even though Clark wasn't downtown, the Sixth and Fourth Wards were still deep. Most of my classmates grew up around each other so we know each other's lives outside of school, too. A lot of times the drama that occurs in school starts in the neighborhoods. I remember when I was younger, everybody's mama used to say, "If somebody hit you, you better hit them back." When girls fight, it's usually over a boy, but when boys fight it's usually over wards. It's stupid to finish a fight off at school when you already know the consequences, but if you gotta fight to defend yourself, do what you gotta do from getting beat up. You can't be scared all your life.

When I was in middle school, kids used to fight with their hands, but nowadays they're using knives and guns. They don't fight fair anymore and a lot of people my age are getting killed. I hear about people getting stabbed and shot over wards, but I never knew anybody who was directly involved. Brandon and his friends were never into stuff like that and Nakia doesn't care about wards, especially since he lives across the river. I didn't think I would ever get caught up in the drama, but these are the stories of how I did.

SHOOTING AT JOHN MCDONOGH SENIOR HIGH

It all started in April 2003. Head was shot at the corner of North Miro and Dumaine. People said that Caveman did it, but who knows, you can't always listen to what the people say. People thought that Caveman killed Head because both of them had had a little beef, but the rumor was that they later on forgot about it and forgave each other

A week later Caveman was shot in the John McDonogh gym. I wasn't there and didn't see it, so I don't know how it happened. I was sitting by the gate at my high school, Clark, during the lunch break, when an undercover cop rolled up and told us to move from by the gate because they just had a shooting at John Mac and someone had been killed. I was hoping that it wasn't anybody that I knew.

I rode the Broad bus home with my friend Brittany, and she came with me to my house. By the time we got to my house most of the television crews had gone away, but there were still many policemen in the area. We were sitting on my porch just a half a block from the school when a white man with a notebook came up to us and started asking us did we know Caveman and Head. He was asking me about Head, because he knew he went to Clark. Not realizing he was a newspaper reporter, we commented on what he had asked us, but it wasn't too much. He kept asking us if we liked Head and we couldn't say anything bad because we really didn't know him that well. The truth was that I would see Caveman every time that I went by my Grandfather's house on Dumaine Street in the Fifth Ward. As for Head, I used to see him at school. I didn't have anything against either one of them. To me they were cool people.

The next day they had a big write-up about the killing that included quotes from myself and Brittany. I couldn't believe how he twisted our words around. The reporter made it like we didn't like Head and Caveman. It was a big mess, and the reporter made more drama.

After the shooting, John Mac got a bad name. Stories about the shooting stayed on the news for weeks and weeks, a big beef grew between the Fifth and Sixth wards, and Brittany and I were caught in between. People kept asking me, "Why you said that about that boy, why you said this?" I would just tell them to mind their business, because everything you read in the newspaper is not true. The conflict got to the point that people were telling me that I should watch out, that people were going to do me something. My mom got worried about me, and Brittany's mom got worried about her, so they pulled us out of school for the rest of the year.

BECOMING A TROJAN

The next year, Clark wouldn't let me back in because they said I wasn't in the district anymore because they had moved downtown. What I couldn't understand was how come when Clark was Uptown I was in the district but now that it's Downtown where I live I'm not in the district.

When I switched schools I really didn't want to go to John Mac but I really didn't have a choice. I was feeling nervous the day before school. I was saying to myself, "People not gonna like me," which didn't make a lot of sense because I already knew a lot of people that went there from middle school. I also thought maybe because of the newspaper article that would cause some more drama since Caveman got shot in the gym.

My first day wasn't like when you be in elementary and your mama brings you to school and walk to your class. I was all on my own. A friend of mine came got me that morning and we walked to school together. I got bubble guts when I first walked in the building and saw everybody looking all fresh with brand new everything. Boys with new haircuts and girls wearing roller wraps and braids.

My first day was better than I thought it was going to be. It didn't take long for me to adjust because my friend showed me around. I saw a lot of people I hadn't seen since elementary. They said, "You shoulda been came here in the first place."

Now that this is my second year at John Mac, I'm straight. I don't have nothing to worry about. I am familiar with a lot of people and a lot of people are familiar with me. Sometimes, I think, too familiar because everybody knows where I live. People ask, "Don't you stay right there?" You never know, one of my teachers might come and knock on my door. Now I can show the new students around because I know how it feels to be lost and don't know where anything is.

Pretend you're a new student and I will take you on a tour of my school. There are good and bad things about John Mac. Entering John Mac every one uses the door on the Dorgenois Street side. Walk in the gate and someone is asking to see our ID. No ID, no school. You get checked by a security guard before you can go in the building. John Mac has a first, second, and third floor. The first floor is mainly freshman and special ed. Tenth through twelfth graders are on the second and third floor. As you walk down the hall you see educational things on the walls. Students walk the halls knowing that they are supposed to be in class. Inside one of the girls' restrooms, you see lots of graffiti on the stalls and walls. In some classrooms, the graffiti is just out of control. Most of the graffiti says Third Ward, Fourth Ward, Sixth Ward, Seventh Ward—stuff that doesn't even make sense.

John Mac has some good teachers and some not so good ones. John McDonogh High to work on their pride. The class conditions are very poor and the students don't make it better. Even though John Mac is not the best-looking school in the world, but it's my school and I'm not ashamed of it, not one bit of it. I'm always going to represent my school no matter what.

People don't know the real John Mac. John Mac isn't all that bad, but when someone does have a fight, the next thing you know the news people are filming the camera trying to make us look bad. Yup, they be putting us on beam when they show us on the news and you know they just tell their side of the story.

BRANDON AND THE POLICE

Brandon and Mike went to Clark together one morning. They parked Mike's car on the far side of the school and rather than walking all the way around to get in the school the right way, they went through a little hole that was near their parking spot. Nobody was supposed to go through the hole, but students still did to avoid going all the way around.

Mike and Brandon got caught, and were suspended for three days. On day two of his suspension, Brandon was sitting at home bored, and decided to go outside by his friends on Bayou Road. He got on his bike, and rode down the Dorgenois sidewalk. He rode past John Mac to the corner of Esplanade. A policeman approached him, and told him to get off the bike. Before he could, the policeman punched him in the chest and pushed him down on the ground. He started beating Brandon, and all of the John Mac students were standing around watching because school was just letting out.

Word got to our mama fast, because our house is so close to the school. My mother went to see what was going on with Brandon as I was getting off the Broad bus. People were telling me that the police had beaten up my brother. I ran home, but my mother was up by John Mac. When I got there I saw Brandon cuffed to the a chair like he was some type of criminal.

I couldn't control myself. Man, I was going off, saying, "My brother didn't do nothing! Man, that's messed up!"

Then I just left because I started crying. I didn't want to see my bother with bruises on his head and arms and a busted lip. My mama went off on the police that had beaten him up, but they still brought Brandon to jail and charged him with mandatory school attendance, resisting arrest, and trespassing.

Okay, he couldn't have been trespassing, because school had already let out. Plus, he was riding the bike on the sidewalk, minding his own business. The reason he wasn't in school is because he was suspended. And I know that he is not stupid enough to resist arrest by a police officer. Wherever that police officer is, he knows deep down that he was wrong.

PART III: THE BLOCK

When I first heard I was going to have to do interviews with my neighbors on North Dorgenois, I told my teachers, "I don't know them people!" My family was friendly with some of the neighbors, but in general it's a quiet block and people stay mainly to themselves. I was nervous and I didn't know how people would react when I asked them to be a part of my book. At first, they wanted to know, "What do you want to interview me for?" But when I told them more about the project, they started to be more interested and said they would participate.

Through the interviews, I learned how nice my neighbors are and how a lot of them had been on the block for years and years. I thought that they wanted to stick with the people they knew, but they were all cool and supportive. I learned that not everybody thinks the same way as people my age do about the Sixth Ward. Most people said they liked the houses on our street and how close they are to Esplanade. Some agreed that it was a little boring, but thought it was a good thing. Others thought it wasn't boring enough.

MRS. MARCELLA

Mrs. Marcella's house is the left house on my side. It's pink, big and has an upstairs and downstairs. I've been in there twice. I can't remember how many bedrooms it has, but it's a lot. Mrs. Marcella is an older lady, about sixty-five years old. She owns her house and she's been there at least thirty years.

Mrs. Marcella has been raising two foster children. Yara is in her late twenties and Jazel is thirty-something. Both of them are special, which means they need extra attention and extra watching. Yara has light skin with freckles and is kind of heavy-set. Jazel is more the quiet type. She just stares or stands on the porch and rocks and probably makes a little humming noise. She is tall with light brown skin and hazel eyes. If you see her, you would think she could not read, but she can.

You know how some old people just be mean and nosey at the same time? Mrs. Marcella will tell you straight up that she is nosey. She likes to talk about people on the block. She loves little children. She calls the little kids her little grandbabies.

My mother is close to her. I told my mama if she talks about other people to you, she probably talks about you to other neighbors, you never know. Mrs. Marcella is getting older and can't get around that well, so my mama goes to the store for her. She doesn't mind because she knows Mrs. Marcella is unable. Sometimes she'll be sitting on the porch in a chair and can barely get up. My mama says, "She good for it. She cool people."

One day Mrs. Marcella wanted Yara to go to the store and my mama said, "Ebony, why don't you go with Yara to the store?" I wanted to say no, but that would have been rude. When we walked to the store, all eyes were on us. I felt so stupid. Yara walked too fast, and at the store she was embarrassing me acting all loud and common. She was in one line and I was in the other. A boy got in front of her and she didn't say anything until the boy left of the store. A man asked her, "Why you didn't say anything?" and Yara said, "I would have had to kick his ass." Yara claims she's going to have a baby, but I don't think she can.

I remember at one time my mama and Ms. Marcella were not speaking to each other because Ms. Marcella had accused Brandon and his friends of stealing her big heavy iron gates off her porch and on the side of the house. I think it was a rockhead or someone who was desperate for money. My brother and his friends all have jobs and don't have time to be playing around with gates. Ms. Marcella started talking to my mama again first. But my mama had told her not to be accusing people if she couldn't prove it.

Ms. Marcella lived alone with Yara and Jazel, but after awhile, her birth daughter—Stephanie—moved in with her daughter and grandchildren. Yara started to feel jealous, like she wasn't getting enough attention. When I would pass by the house, I overheard her talking to herself saying she wanted Stephanie and her family to leave and move into their own house because she was sick of them.

One morning a couple of days later I walked outside to check the mailbox and I saw the police by Mrs. Marcella's house. The first thing I said to myself was, "Now, what happened over there?" The police were talking to Yara outside on the porch. She looked very upset. The police put Yara in the car and took her away.

The next day, my mom and I were sitting on the porch chillin' when Mrs. Marcella's granddaughter Tiffany came over to explain the lil' incident that happened. Tiffany said Yara was trying to stab Ms. Marcella with an ice pick.

Yara was gone for a long time. She really wanted to come home but she couldn't. The first day Ms.

Marcella let her come back, she was sitting on the porch again.

As I was doing my interviews, I wanted to talk to Mrs. Marcella more about the experience, but she became sick. Over the last few months, she has been in and out of the hospital. Yara and Gazell are gone. If I'm not mistaken, I think her daughter is going to put her in a home and sell the house.

INTERVIEW WITH TIM JACKSON

I used to see Mr. Tim outside sweeping and washing his truck. Mrs. Marcella told us that his mother shared a house with him, but that's about all I knew about him. When I asked him if he wanted to do an interview, he said, "Yeah, sure."

I learned that he's a good builder. He built a small building in his backyard that he rents out for parties or to people who are in town temporarily. It was set up with a bed, TV, radio, telephone, bathroom, and a little kitchen. He also renovated part of his house that he showed me during the interview. Now when I see Mr. Tim, I make sure I speak to him and show my appreciation. He always asks me how my book is coming along.

Ebony: Where did you grow up?

Tim: I grew up in the Ninth Ward right around St. Roch.

E: What do you do for a living?

T: I work at a hotel. I set up for banquet meetings and conventions. I'll be out of work for a little while because I'm about to have surgery. I had surgery on this leg once, and now I'm about to have surgery on this one. The job consists of a lot of walking and lifting, so that's a lot of wear and tear on your body.

E: Describe the block for someone who hasn't been here before.

T: It's a quiet block, not a lot of traffic. The only time they really had a lot of traffic was when the school let out or when they're going to school. You don't have too many kids that stay in the block. Mostly middle-aged people.

E: How do you feel about living on the same block as a church?

T: It's good because on one side of the street, I don't have to worry about neighbors being on that side. Not too many people stay in this block because of the church, you know. It takes up a lot space where houses would be.

E: How long have you been living here?

T: About fifteen years. My house is a four-plex. It's stressful [being a landlord] for the simple fact that I have so many different people. One time I had a young lady staying back here. She moved her boyfriend in and I came in and there are a couple of guys on that corner and some guys here and they knew my name. "We're

staking out the place." They had policemans all on the side of the house, laying down on the ground and all that, waiting for him to come back home. On the other side, the tenant wanted to move her boyfriend in, [and he turned out to be] abusive. Constantly fighting and fighting. I had to replace the back door.

E: Has the block changed?

T: Well, it's basically the same. Most people who live in this block are homeowners.

COMMUNITY AND SAFETY

E: How well do you know your neighbors?

T: I know just about everybody in the block.

E: Who are you closest to on the block or in the neighborhood?

T: Well, I'm real close to Ms. Marcella.

E: What is your relationship with her like?

T: We talk and conversate about what's going on in the neighborhood and she tell me about her family and I tell her about my family and we keep an eye out for each other.

E: Do you spend any time outside?

T: Most of the time I'm outside sweeping up, picking up a little trash or some thing like that. That's about it.

E: Do you feel safe?

T: Yes. You have a lot of policeman coming back and forth from here. Crime is not bad in this neighborhood. To me, it's not.

E: Do you think this would be a good neighborhood to raise your children in?

T: Yes. This neighborhood is laid-back. You know, I sit on the porch, watch the cars pass by. I have one child—he's eight. He don't stay with me, though. He stay with his mother. For a young person it would be boring. My little boy don't like comin over cuz there's nothing to do. "Daddy, there's nothing to do but look at TV and go outside and run around."

INVESTMENT

E: What is your most powerful memory of the block?

T: I can remember one time they had a big party over there in the hall across the street by the church, and they came out and second lined all in the street with a band. My brother is into a lot of that. He used to be in Jolly Bunch and he's in the Men of Olympics or something like that. I never was into that kind of stuff. I just can't see myself putting the money out, but to each his own. It's just not me.

I don't go out too much. In my younger days I used to go all the clubs and hang out, but as you get older I've got everything I need here: stereo, movies. I do a lot of reading on home improvements, you know, a lot of building things. I built this entertainment cabinet myself and I just recently finished a project in the back. I built a studio apartment and a friend [and I] are going to rent it out for baby showers, Jazz Fest, maybe Bayou Classic and Mardi Gras.

I wanted to branch out and buy more houses, but I said no. I'm just gonna stay here. Right now, it's cool. I'm reaping the benefits, you know. I bought it for like $35,000. And when I refinanced it, it was worth a $130,000. If I ever meet a woman I want to marry, we'll buy a bigger one. And this will basically pay for where we live at.

INTERVIEW WITH THELMA SANDERS

Ms. Thelma lives on the corner of Barracks and North Dorgenois. She's a nice lady. I usually see her in the evening cleaning up by blowing leaves or sweeping. Every time, I speak. Ms. Thelma is a more inside person, but when she gets to talking with my mother they don't know how to stop. This interview is the first time I had a long conversation with her. She said she really enjoyed it and I did, too.

Ebony: Where did you grow up? How is it different than North Dorgenois?

Thelma: I grew up in the St. Bernard Housing Project. The St. Bernard neighborhood was overcrowded. Any housing complex is going to be overrun with people [and] when you have a lot of people flowing out onto the street, there's a lot of confusion. The difference between there and here is that—again—you have a place to grow.

E: What do you do for a living now—or what did you do for a living?

T: I'm retired after nearly forty years of being a dry-cleaning presser.

E: When you first came into the neighborhood, did you like it?

T: Yes, I did. I came in on a Saturday and it was rather quiet and that's why I liked it.

E: Describe the block for someone who has never been there before.

T: The sounds that you're hearing in the background now are what this neighborhood is like. You hear church bells at a distance, traffic at a distance. No real outside activity, and this goes on year round.

E: How long have you been living here?

T: Nearly twelve years.

E: How has it changed?

T: The neighborhood itself hasn't changed. The only thing that has really changed is the people who rent some of the houses. The only thing that's changed has been the faces.

E: If you could move where would you go?

T: Well, let's see. I would probably move some place out of the city. But, really, I hadn't thought about moving anywhere. I like where I am.

E: How long do you plan to stay here?

T: Probably for the rest of my life.

E: Why would you move?

T: If the crime rate became greater in this area. If the noise level became any higher—those would be two reasons for me moving.

E: Do the children bother you when school lets out?

T: Not at all.

E: How do you feel about living close to a high school?

T: I enjoy listening to the music, watching the band march up and down the street. They usually don't stay too late. They don't do it too loud. I rather enjoy it. It brings me back.

E: How well do you know your neighbors?

T: Oh, well enough.

E: Who are you closest to on the block or in the neighborhood?

T: I would say that the person I'm closest to is Henrietta Bolding.

E: Do you spend anytime outside?

T: Not much, not a whole lot. I'm an inside person. I'm not your regular native New Orleanian. I don't relate to sitting outside on the porch.

E: Do you feel safe?

T: Absolutely.

E: What makes you feel safe in the neighborhood? What doesn't?

T: I've got a gun. Not being able to locate that gun makes me feel not safe.

E: What is the most powerful memory of your block?

T: The unfortunate incident that took place a couple of years ago with the John McDonogh student being killed in the gym. Now, while that was really something to remember, the way that the press and the media tried to milk it that was the most memorable thing.

E: Do you have any important life events that happened in your life?

T: Both good and bad.

INTERVIEW WITH
TIM AND LAURA SCHNEIDER

For many years, two old white men lived in the big house across the street from me. When they put the house up for sale, it stayed on the market for a loooong time. They had to bring the price down because no one was interested in paying that much. It was eventually bought by a doctor and his pregnant wife. They were nice, but I didn't see them too much because he was always at work and she stayed inside.

Ebony: Where did you grow up?

Laura: In Annapolis, Maryland, which is very, very suburban.

Tim: I grew up in a planned community called Columbia, Maryland, which is also very suburban planning.

L: Annapolis is really preppy and conservative.

E: How is it different than North Dorgenois?

L: Just about every way.

T: It's very different, the suburban versus urban— you know, there's housing projects only three or four blocks from here. We had low-income housing in Columbia but not the scale of the large project out here, and the economics are different. Things that both Annapolis and uh, Columbia have a lot higher income.

L: They're relatively affluent communities.

T: I think that the neighborhood is more racially diverse. Actually, where I grew up it was probably about 25% black and 10% Latino, and there was a large Asian population there and maybe 60% white, whereas here—it's predominantly black because New Orleans is 85% black. So that's very different.

E: What do the both of you do for a living?

T: I'm a doctor and my wife is a stay-at-home mom.

L: Before that I was the associate director of an art gallery.

NORTH DORGENOIS

E: When you first came into the neighborhood, did you like it?

T: We had been renting so it was really nice to have our own home. We were right in the middle of the city and so it took some getting used to.

L: We didn't realize that the band practiced in the middle of the street!

E: Describe the block for someone who hasn't been here before.

L: I would call it pretty much a typical urban community. It's transitional. There are older people, people with kids, there are people of all different races, there are people of different economic backgrounds, there's a church, there's a school, so there's a lot of activity of street.

T: New Orleans has a lot of block-to-block variation. This block has a lot of a lot of variation within it. We have a large single-family home and right next-door there are apartments for rent. There are duplexes, there are buildings divided into apartments.

L: It's a beautiful block, though. I mean, the architecture is really nice and we have beautiful live oaks going down our street.

E: How do you feel about living on the same block as a church?

L: It's nice to hear the church bells.

E: Do the children bother you when school lets out?

T: As a rule, no. I think all kids are boisterous when they get out of school and I think that's normal. The only thing that bothers me is probably two or three kids with their horns, that blow the horns in the middle of the street.

L: They're not even playing the horn.

T: They're not even playing the music—they're just blaring one note over and over again right in front of the house. It's almost like they're trying to make me crazy—but I wouldn't say "the" children, I would say those particular children.

L: And like with having a baby—

T: When Greta was little and she would sleep all through the day, it would wake her. In general, they are not as noisy as I thought they would be.

L: Yeah, [one of the] two men who used to live here said he used to have a real problem. I don't know if the school has talked to the kids.

E: How do you feel about living close to a high school?

T: That was terrible to know that there was a shooting right across the street.

COMMUNITY, SAFETY, VIOLENCE

E: How well do you know your neighbors?

L: Because I'm here more, I probably know the neighbors better than Tim does. We know the neighbors that live on either side. They're renovating next to us, but we have met them. [We know] the people next door, and we're friendly with you and your mom, and the woman who lives in your double. Oh, and Ms. Marcella, but other than that—I don't know any of our neighbors, like down the street. There's not a real sense of community here, I guess. You don't really meet your neighbors very much in the street. People aren't hanging out.

E: Do you spend any time outside?

T: In the yard. I mean, not in the street or anything. I mean, we work raking leaves and things like that.

L: We walk down Esplanade. We walk to Whole Foods and walk over to the video place a lot.

E: What is your most powerful memory of the block?

L: Bringing my newborn baby home, probably, and your mom was outside. That really felt like a neighborhood because they were excited for us, you know. We brought the baby home—that was a really happy time for us.

E: Do you feel safe?

T: Reasonably so.

L: Yeah, I feel safe here.

E: What makes you feel safe in the neighborhood? What doesn't?

T: Well, we have an alarm system and a security fence, which are those obvious things. They're kind of superficial but they—and a dog—they make me feel safe. Just anywhere in a city, I think that would make you feel safe.

L: Neighbors sitting out. Like you and your mom a lot and Ms. Marcella is out a lot and so I think that makes me feel a little safer. Things that don't make me feel safe is sometimes the church will have an activity—a wedding or something—and people getting a little out of hand. Which is strange, because like I said, I thought it would be neat to have a church on the street. You have the church bells, the pretty things—the ceremonies and then you have this craziness at the same time. And then there have been shootings on this street. Since we've lived here there have been at least three.

T: On the other side of Esplanade there have been three shootings in three years.

L: This side of Esplanade, honey, that body was found right here.

T: So, that makes me feel unsafe—finding dead bodies.

L: The police come when you call them—that makes me feel safer. They take a little while, but they—

T: We've heard a certain amount of gunshots, but maybe we're just jaded.

L: We lived in DC.

T: We lived in DC for a while and we used to hear gunshots almost every night.

E: Do you think this would be a good neighborhood to raise your children in?

L: Mmm....

T: Yes and no. It's got its good sides and its down sides. The gun violence—that's not a good way to raise a child. That's a very big no. But at the same time, there are very sweet, good people here, and it's close to a lot of nice things, good things. You know, I'm really torn.

L: Living in the city, like Tim said, is such a double-edged sword. I want my daughter to know different cultures. I want her to know that there are lots of different people in the world and there's so many experiences I want her to have. I don't want her to live in some little, you know, vacuum somewhere and not understand. You know, any city, but particularly New Orleans, I think it's great. But I worry. It's tough, you know, raising kids anywhere, but in a city when there's this much violence—even if you are not looking for trouble somehow it finds you sometimes. Raising kids, I would worry not about this block or this community but anywhere in the city.

MOVING

E: If you could move where would you go?

T: Well, we are going to move. We're moving back home to where we can be near our families in Maryland.

E: What will be some of your favorite memories?

T: This is my first home and it's the place where I lived when my daughter was born. I think this is always going to be memorable for that reason.

L: Yeah, but I think some of our favorite memories will be of our home in this community.

BOARDED UP

The house is peach and white with boards on the window and a black fence. There's an oak tree on the corner and lots of leaves around the gate. I'm thinking about when the black couple used to stay there and got put out. Now a couple—both doctors—bought the house and had it fixed. There's a rumor that they are taking the workers to court because they don't like the finished work. My mother and Tammi saw in the inside of the house and said it was converted to a single. The only time we see the couple is when they come and pick up their mail.

INTERVIEW WITH SANDRA EWELL

The house on the corner of North Dorgenois and Governor Nicholls was bad. It was all broken up and the roof was falling in. It was abandoned and I never thought anyone would ever live there again. But as years passed by, it was slowly looking better. I never knew who was fixing it up, but I would see a woman pull up in a red truck to work on it. Sometimes little children would help her. Still, no one was living there and I didn't think I would get an interview for the book. One day, though, I went over there and some men were working on the house. They said she would be back in the next half an hour and I caught her then.

Ebony: Why did you pick this house?

Sandra: Well, I own a home two blocks down right across the street from Bethany Nursing Home. My mother came to visit me one day and brought me in front of this particular house. Now, Governor Nicholls used to be called Hospital Street. My mother lived on Hospital Street. We stood right in front of this house and she showed me where she lived with her parents in the early 1900s. She loved this neighborhood. So Governor Nicholls, which is what it's called now, was very important to me because this was where my mother was raised. [We] were very, very close. I always wanted a house right in this little area.

One day I was riding my bike and [I saw that] this house [was] on the market. It was only six thousand dollars. The roof was open, but what remained of it was full of cypress. I had a guy to come and dismantle the two top stories. Actually, I gutted the whole house. The only thing I kept from this house is the front. I kept the structure, the windows, but the only actual part that stood was the front wall. The foundation was just terrible. It had to be completely leveled [and] it had to be reframed. I've been working on this house for four years. It's been taking a long time because I keep running out of money.

A year ago, I was riding my bike on Esplanade Avenue. I was going to the French Quarter and a big SUV hit me on my bike so it broke my leg in three places. I had to stop working on my house and recuperate, so it's been a year [but] now I'm back on renovating.

I'm in the process of making this into a very interesting, comfortable little Creole cottage. This house was listed in the New Orleans register of historic homes, cause it was originally built in 1896. The grandchildren of the man who built [it] came and talked to me. They're very interested in seeing it refurbished and [want it to] stay as [close to the original structure] as possible. I have changed some things, but I've tried to keep the windows the same; the floor plan inside is basically the same, [too].

E: What kind of neighborhood did you grow up in?

S: Actually, I grew up in the lower Ninth Ward. It was fourteen of us and it was very reasonable then to buy a home. My father and mother bought two lots. They paid five hundred dollars apiece for the lots and my father built our house himself. It was all they could afford then because things were so hard. We were all taught to buy a house, build a house, own a home. Consequently, all of us own numerous houses. This is about the fifth one [for me]. I live in em, I fix em up, and move on.

E: What are your plans for this house? Do you plan to live here or rent it out?

S: Definitely live here. My house two blocks down is on the market. Hopefully, by the time my house sells, this one will be ready and I'll just move in here.

E: What do think is important in a neighborhood?

S: Cleanliness, cooperation with the neighbors. The reason I chose this neighborhood is because I like for the property that I'm renovating to be like a model for the rest of the neighbors. I could have picked a house [in] a higher-priced neighborhood, but I like to kind of set a precedent. The other neighbors can see what I'm doing. I usually do a lot of landscaping. I put a lot of flowers, a lot of pretty plants and usually people in the neighborhood start catching on and everyone starts fixing up their property.

E: So do you do landscaping for a living?

S: Yeah, you could say that. I really am limited now because of my leg being hurt. Mainly my income is from buying houses. Fixing em up. Sell em. I usually sell a house every two years and that's where I make my living.

I have one son and he's twenty-three. He always said that he hated construction but I bribed him, encouraged him, begged him to work with me and he learned how to fix houses up. He learned some things from working with me and now he's building with my brother. Hopefully he'll follow my footsteps, cause Jesus was a builder and I think for a man to be a builder is a very blessed vocation. It's a good thing for a man work with his hands. He feels good about himself, can build his own home and build other houses for people.

New Orleans is a historic city and we have so many beautiful houses here. Our young people need to know that they can buy houses very reasonable. You can buy a house in New Orleans [for] under 20,000. You can invest 10-20,000 to fix it up, live in it comfortably, and then you can sell it for twice, three times that amount of money. You walked away with a nice chunk of money and you've lived comfortably. You feel good about yourself because you own your own property.

Abram: Ebony used to live here on Dorgenois, and now she lives on Dumaine.

S: Moved? Did you like Dorgenois?

E: No.

S: I know. There's drugs sold here.

E: It's too quiet.

S: It's too quiet? [Laughing]. I own some land in Mississippi and ooh, Mississippi is quiet. This is not quiet

to me at all. It's noisy. There are a lot of kids, but that's okay, you know, because I think kids need an example. When the kids in the neighborhood ask me can they work, I never refuse them because I know that they have to learn and I like for them to want to work. I'm happy to teach them and let them work and make a few dollars.

In fact, I'm in the process to start a landscape club at John Mac. I worked with [the last principal] Mr. Goodwin—he and I went to high school together— and did some landscaping at John McDonogh.

INTERVIEW WITH MS. ARTHE IVORY

Ms. Ivory moved to the block with her fiancé and daughter less than a year ago. She lives in the back apartment in a pink house across the street from me. My mom got friendly with her because they used to catch the Esplanade bus together in the morning. They swapped stories about the neighborhood and let each other know if something was going on. When I interviewed her, it sounded like she missed her old neighborhood a lot. We agreed that people should get to know each other more.

Ebony: Where did you grow up?

Ms. Ivory: I was raised up uptown in the Thirteenth Ward. I lived in a shotgun that was a three-bedroom dwelling.

E: What did your parents do for a living?

I: My mother was a teacher and my grandmother was a cook for the school board. Basically, I was raised by a matriarchal family. All females. My grandfather died in '69. From '69 on up until maybe two or three years ago, she ran everything. Whatever she said went.

My grandmother was from the country, very much old-fashioned girl. She was a Creole—very bright, long hair. She spoke French, and my aunties spoke French—they also spoke pig latin and something.

But I don't speak it. I keep her picture up [on the wall. She lived there for 30 years, then they moved to Algiers Point across the River, then they moved uptown on Roberts Street where she lived 50 some years in the same house.

I'm an only child. My mother attended Dillard University – she was an education major—and she got pregnant with me in her senior year. She didn't want any kids. She always said, "I didn't want any kids, but here you come." After she had me, I often asked her, "Why did you just have one child?" She said, "Well, I just needed one blessing —I didn't need all these kids." She had a sister and [my aunt] Lorraine had four kids. You'd see all these people coming from my house—they were my cousins. We were all raised up together cuz when my mom and my auntie taught during the day, we would all go to my grandmother's house in the evening. First thing: homework. Second thing: you eat. TV was not permitted.

We read books. We had to write articles about the newspaper—just pick an article out the paper and write about it. We had a little Bible session. Then, daylight permitted, we went out to play. I raised my kids the same way. They followed in my footsteps— no babies, no drugs, no jail, you know. They turned out to be pretty good.

My grandmother was ninety-eight when she died. She was in Bethany Home for two years. I walked over there everyday. And when she died, it was just unbelievable. My mother had a nervous breakdown. She had been with her mother all her life. She never got married, never left the nest. So when my grandmother took sick, I think it had an effect on her.

She's in a home now on Franklin Avenue called the Harmony House. And she's got schizoparanoia, which means she hears voices, so she has to take medicine daily. But she's doing fine.

It was really a battle ever since I was a small girl; I think I was about nine when I first saw the reaction—she would just tear up stuff and would be talking to herself in the back of the house—didn't keep jobs. I was afraid of her because, at that time, I didn't know what schizoparanoia was. My grandmother committed her to the third floor of Charity, which was the mental ward. She stayed there on and off for about four or five years. When she came out, I was in junior high school. From maybe seventh grade up until two years ago she was fine. When my grandmother took sick, I think she knew that nothing was ever gonna be the way it was [and] it really took its toll on her.

E: What is it you do for a living?

I: I have two degrees. I went into education because all of my family was in education. I stopped teaching at Samuel J. Peters—that's Israel Augustine on Broad and Tulane.

E: Why did you stop?

I: It was just some kids. They were kind of rowdy. I guess their parents weren't spending time with them—just a lost generation. I was bringing them clothes and containers of breakfast. [One of the boys] got mad one day. I told him he had to leave. He came back and said, "Miss Ivory." He had a big cup of something, I didn't know what it was until I smelled it on me. He said something like, "You're going to burn in hell" and before he could throw the match I slapped his hand. I just decided "No, this is not for me." About two years later, I found out he was being abused. His mom was drinking and drugging. These kids were basically raising themselves.

I said, "I'm going to find another major." So I went back to Delgado and took up electronic training and I did most of the installs for the casinos. But I left the casino alone because I was working until like three and four o'clock in the morning, and [my daughter] was home by herself [and] my son was working. So I changed and I went to Public Storage and I've been there ever since. Three or four years ago, [the boy who tried to light me on fire] came in with his wife to Public Storage. He didn't know me cuz my hair used to be really long and I was much smaller. When I told him who I was he just started crying at the counter. I was like, "Hey, you've done good." He went to college. He's got a family, and they're living across the lake somewhere.

I'm planning on leaving and going back to school to do something else when [my daughter's finished [with college]. It's probably going to be something in electronics, cuz I like fixing old things and working on electronic pieces.

E: Where were you staying before you came to North Dorgenois?

I: I lived at 1522 North Dupre Street, and I stayed there for nine years. It's a real busy little area. The bank was on that side [of North Broad Street], the cleaners was on that side, CC's Coffee was on that side. During jazz fest we used to just walk over there. The reason I moved to Dorgenois is because my landlord died. She lived next door to me. Her daughters came from the hospital on September the 29th and told me their mother passed. They weren't from New Orleans and they were going to put the house up for sale.

I started looking to buy the house, but it had a lot of termite damage. I knew that if we bought it we would have to spend 80 or 100,000 dollars just to redo it. I was like, "No, it's not worth it."

E: Why did you pick this neighborhood?

I: My fiancé and I started walking and canvassing the neighborhood. We came here and I met Ms. Evelyn Folk— the owner of this house—and I talked to her. We went to the bank and got the money, came back, and a month later we moved in.

E: How is this neighborhood different or similar to your other one?

I: Well, it's different because on that side of Broad it was basically more homeowners. I got to know everyone [in] a three-block radius from where I stayed because I had been there so many years. It was a mixed race of people. [There were] Mexicans across the street, my landlord was Irish; the lady who lived on the other half of the double was from Denmark, and I met two other girls that were from Alaska. We all knew each other. We would get picnics and go in each other's yard. We had gardens with peppers and all kind of stuff, and we'd share it. I had a two-hundred year old pecan tree [and] we would go out there and pick the pecans and make praline candy. I miss that.

[Here], I don't even know my neighbors in the front [of the house]. You know, we speak, and that's it. I met Tiffany and your mom at the bus stop. Basically everybody around here has cars, and we don't have a car. When we get to know each other, we look out for each other. It's just a different world on this side. I pass [my old] house all the time and just look at it and get tears in my eyes like, "Oh my God, I can't believe I'm out of there." So, here I am.

E: What is important to you in a neighborhood?

I: I think that you should get to know your neighbors and familiarize yourself with the area. I'm from a very old fashion family, and we spoke to our neighbors. As a matter of fact, we knew every last one of them. Here, I don't know maybe two people on the block. There's a doctor who lives next door. I don't know [his name], I just know he's a doctor. He'll wave but I rarely see him. I think its just important that you get to know your neighbors.

E: Describe the block to someone who has never been here before.

I: Well, this block is nice. I don't like living in the back [of a house], you know. I'm used to living on the front where I can see everything, so I have floodlights all on the side. My daughter's in college. She goes out and comes in at different hours. God forbid if something should happen. So, I like to keep it well lit.

It doesn't flood over here and there's nice oak trees. I noticed there's a sofa out there, there's a desk across the street from the school that has been there six weeks. And I don't know why they don't pick it up. On Dupre you put anything out and it was gone. So I'm gonna call the sanitation department cuz they need to pick it up.

E: Would you call this neighborhood the Sixth Ward?

I: Dorgenois Street. The ward thing is more or less with the younger generation. Basically I know wards by voting polls. I don't even know what ward this is. You say the Sixth Ward? Oh, okay. Well, you told me something I didn't know. I don't even know what ward it is on that side. We just called it Dupre Street.

E: Do you feel safe in your neighborhood?

I: Sometimes. And sometimes is when I come home straight from work, I don't go back outside. If it's dark, I don't go out because I don't know anybody around here.

The day I moved in, there was a murder across the street from John Mac, and I was going to catch the bus. The guy that I catch the bus with everyday, Solomon—that was his wife. She left Tastee Donuts and was going home when somebody followed her and shot her in the back and killed her. I saw the crime tape and the police and the paramedics. I walked over two blocks and when I saw her laying on the ground, I was just blown away. I was like, "Oh my god, what is going on?" I came back home, I told my fiancée and my daughter, "We got to get out of here." He said "Baby, that's isolated."

I found out something was going on with her and some of the neighbors on [the other side of Esplanade]. She knew the people who followed her from Tastee [Donut]. As a matter of fact, the young lady who was killed's uncle works at Craig with your mother. Your mom found out about it cuz I told her about it at the bus stop. So she said, "Oh yeah, I know the girl." Your mother said that it's quiet around here, things like that don't happen and didn't happen on this side, but about a week after that I heard gunshots. I was like freaking out in here.

E: How do you feel about the school?

I: The school John Mac, down the street? You have John Mac students passing all the time, in the mornings and the evenings, the band playing. I really don't have a use for it.

Like I say, I am from a very religious old family. I'm very disgusted and amazed that when I catch the bus at the corner of Dorgenois and Esplanade, we encounter children with vulgar, vulgar mouths. The guys pants hanging off, and trying to put their shirts in their pants.

I've noticed that you all have to wear black and white shoes. The girls are coming with pink, green shoes on, and they're turning them around at the gate and sending them home. My concern is that you're sending them home, but do the parents know they're being sent home? Are they going home? I heard the principle talk in the morning, telling them, "You cannot wear these different colored shoes."

When Caveman was killed at the school, I was at work. A friend of mine called me and said, "What school is your daughter going to?" She said, "Oh my God, there's shooting at John Mac." When I got home that evening, and I saw the news, I just cried. Thet guy who did the shooting lived next door to us on Dupre when I first moved into the house. His mother worked at a hotel downtown. She had maybe six or seven kids. He would take and steal bicycles and stuff and would bring them through the alley. One night my daughter, my cousin Shawndra, and I walked to Tastee Donuts. He came up behind us and was getting ready to rob us. When I turned around, he saw who I was and just kind of rolled off. But the next day I saw him in the yard and I told him, "You know,

I don't know what was your purpose last night." He said, "Oh no, we weren't trying to do nothing. We were trying to holla at your daughter." No, you wasn't. You was up to no good.

I said this is a shame this is going on in the schools. I was glad when they tore down the hanger in the back and they're checking you all at the gate. You gotta have security in the schools nowadays. When I went to school, it wasn't that way. Times have changed.

E: How long do you plan to stay here?

I: Not long. My lease is up here in October, and I'll probably start looking again. The house is okay, it's just that we came from three bedrooms, and a lot of my stuff is in storage. My sofa and all of that can't fit in here. I will probably go back where I came from, on the other side, in that area.

INTERVIEW WITH BOSWELL ATKINSON

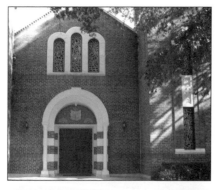

When people are getting out of church, I'm just waking up. They walk by on their way to their vehicles while I'm standing on the porch. The old ladies walking by dressed in their suits with pumps, leaving behind their scent of perfume. The little girls and boys dressed in their lace dresses, pants and bow ties. They look so cute and handsome.

People who attend the church live all over the city. There are a lot of people from the Caribbean who go there. To learn more about the church and what it's like in Jamaica, I interviewed Mr. Boswell Atkinson.

Mr. Boswell owns a Jamaican restaurant on South Broad Street. He goes to the church on my block. He has a funny accent; you have to really listen to understand what he's saying. He fixed me a big plate of Jamaican food with jerk chicken, curry chicken, callaloo, and rice and peas. I was like, "Man, what this is?" But when I ate it, I really liked it.

MR. BOSWELL

I was born in Hanover, Jamaica, but I grew up in Montego Bay. Jamaicans are a very proud people. Hard working. And I guess that's most people in the world, really, but they say Jamaicans are some of the hardest workin people in the world. They love to have fun, too.

My dad ran a service station and my mom was working in the hotel industry. My dad died in 1983. My mom moved to the Bronx by herself to look for better opportunities. We had a whole lot of cousins and friends in New York, so she didn't have a problem adapting. In New York, there is an extremely large Caribbean population.

I moved to New York to live with my mom and went to college at the New York Institute of Technology and the Academy of Aeronomics. It was like I had never left Jamaica! All the food, music, everything we did in Jamaica we did in New York. I did aircraft maintenance and then I got a bachelor's in management.

LIVING IN NEW ORLEANS

I moved to New Orleans in 1978 to work for Lockheed Martin. We settled in New Orleans East because it was close to the company. [Moving from New York] was a shock. I couldn't get the Jamaican food anymore. The stuff that we needed to cook, we couldn't get so it was difficult for a while. In 1986, I got transferred to Baltimore for two years and then came to New Orleans.

When I came back from Baltimore, my wife was attending the church so I joined it. It's unlike Baptist church with a lot of loud singing and clapping— we're not like that. It's calm. [We] burn a lot of incense. It's more like Catholic, but the priest can get married. That's the main difference.

I started a janitorial firm—I bought a janitorial franchise and I did that for awhile and then I opened the restaurant. I used to cook at home and I started looking around [and saw there] was a need for an authentic Jamaican restaurant in New Orleans, so I opened one.

MOVING BACK HOME

Growing up in Jamaica there's a lot of things I didn't see. When we went back for a visit, my wife said, "We're not visiting any relatives, we're not visiting any friends, we're going to stay at a hotel and we're going to do all things that the tourists do." And it was beautiful! We went rafting, we went to Bond's River. I might be partial, but I think it's the most beautiful place in the world. Nice white sand beach. The water is beautiful—different hues of green. You just have to see it to believe it.

Whenever I go home, I don't want to come back. Whenever I go home, I try to figure out a way— "How can I find a way so that I can move back home?" I haven't been able to do it as yet.

ST. LUKE'S EPISCOPAL CHURCH

One cold Sunday morning, Rachel and I went over to St. Luke's. Before the church service started, we saw Mr. Boswell, the Jamaican man. As the service started, members walk down the center aisle of the church singing and holding candles. A young girl was swinging a little kettle thing that had the beautiful scent of incense. Everyone in the pews was standing. Looking around, I saw young and old people. Mainly old. The pastor is Reverend Canon Rex D. Perry.

I was nervous and scared because I was around a lot of people that I didn't know. Mr. Boswell helped Rachel and me find the prayers and songs in the books. My favorite part was when we stood up and sang some church songs. The choir sounded nice and some members sung solos.

After services were over, we introduced ourselves to members of the church. Then we went to get coffee and cake in the reception hall where Nakia and Tammi had their wedding. All the ladies were asking me if I was going to come back next week. One lady told me, "I'm going to come and ring your doorbell and come and get you for church."

PART IV: MOVING

One Sunday morning a few weeks later, there was a knock on our door. I answered and it was Mr. Arthur, our landlord. I was still in my bed clothes and he was dressed in a shorts and sandels with a hat on.

He asked me, "Is your mother there?"

I called my mother and left them alone to talk. Afterwards, my mother came back and said we might have to move.

"Why?"

"Mr. Arthur said he was selling the house."

"I been wanting to move," I said. But my mama was looking a little conflicted, like she's cool with it, and in another way like she doesn't want to move. I had been learning a lot about the block, but it wasn't making me more attached to it. In the next few months, there would be a lot of changes.

MOVING OUT

Finally the moment I have to be waiting for: My mom said, "Ebony, we're moving." I wanted to jump and touch the clouds. I've lived on North Dorgenois for a long time, seven years. It was about time we moved somewhere else. My mom decided it wasn't a bad idea after all. "I had got tired of that big old house, and it was costing me too much utility money. You have to damn near burn the house down trying to keep it warm. I'm serious. The bills were high."

The last couple of days I have been so tired from packing. My mama and I have been doing all the work. My brother Brandon is so lazy he doesn't want to do anything. My mom always tells him, "Boy, you don't have no maids." I always say he gets away with murder.

We've mainly been packing up stuff in boxes. That's some hard work. You don't know all what you have until you move. Well, I was cleaning out my closet and I found a lot of stuff that I had been looking for— that's how junky my closet was. I got my closet straight now. I have a lot of clothes and books that I don't want anymore. I found my old baby dolls in my closet. I was thinking about giving them to Amvets, but I might keep them because you never know they might be worth some money later on down the line. I want to keep them for childhood memories too.

AN INTERVIEW WITH CORY PARKER

Cory is the new owner of my old house on North Dorgenois. He's in the film industry and moved to New Orleans from Texas. He's renovating the side that we stayed on. It looked all tore up. He took the wood panel on the walls down and he took the carpeting up. When I told him that I had been working on a book on the block, he agreed to be interviewed. We sat on the porch. It felt weird to be at my house when it wasn't my house anymore. I thought about how this might be the last time I was over there, but I wasn't too sad about it.

Ebony: When you first came into the neighborhood, did you like it?

Cory: Yes.

E: How do you like your new neighbors?

C: So far, so good. I've had some problems with burglary. My former tenant's side [has been broken into] four times. They stole things I bought to remodel the house: ceiling fans, paint, you name it. If it's there, they were trying to take it.

E: How did you pick this house to buy?

C: It's a beautiful house. It's in what I hope to be a good neighborhood. I hope that this one thing was isolated, and by putting up all the bars, it fixed the problem.

E: What kind of neighborhood did you grow up in?

C: Suburbs in Dallas originally. I graduated from Duncanville and my whole family is from South Dallas.

E: How is it different from here?

C: It's a lot different. I mean, the culture's different. This is the first time I've ever experienced having to bar up my windows.

E: What are your plans with this house? Do you plan to live here or rent it out?

C: I like the neighborhood. I like the house. I like the location and my plan is to rent out one side and live in the other. So I mean, I'm not gonna change that plan. I still feel comfortable here. What I've been told is they like to target construction sites. They're not targeting me. I think they're targeting the fact that there's tools and things going on inside there. That's my hopes, anyway

E: What do you think is important in a neighborhood?

C: I don't know, family, friends. Getting to know the people. Feeling safe. Feeling at home.

A: What brought you to New Orleans?

C: I'm a set dresser [for] films. I do props as well. I worked last summer here, and then I went back to Texas and did work, and then I came back here in October. The union I'm in covers all of Texas and the union here covers, I think, Louisiana and Mississippi.

E: Describe the block for someone who hasn't been here before.

C: I think it has some beautiful houses, some beautiful trees. Everyone I've talked to here has been friendly. I've tried to introduce myself to a few of the neighbors as often as I can. Thelma seems to be a really nice lady and Toni back here seems to be a nice lady. I think she's been there thirty years. The little kids'll come up and just be playing on my porch while I'm sitting here and want to pet my cat. Everyone I have come over just loves the neighborhood.

E: Do the children bother you when school lets out?

C: No, a lot of times I'm gone. It doesn't faze me at all. I mean, I think it clears out pretty quickly.

E: How do you feel about living close to a high school?

C: I didn't have any hesitations about that. When I first looked at the house, I went over and talked to the security guard. She actually told me not to buy it. She told me, "I wouldn't buy over here." And then I told her it was just right here and she goes, "Oh, well, maybe right there. But just don't buy down there."

E: Do you feel safe?

C: All along I've had a little bit of paranoia with the break-ins, but I still feel safe. I don't feel threatened, [and] I think I've resolved that problem with them coming in. It was just something I had to deal with— a first time experience.

THE LADY WITH THE DOG

While I'm sitting on my old porch, a lady from around the corner passes walking her dog. She stops and shares her feelings about the block. She says that when you're living in this neighborhood make sure you have bars on your windows and big dogs in your house. From my point of view you don't need all of that. When we stayed on North Dorgenois no one ever broke in our house. We never had any problems.

REFLECTIONS ON D-BLOCK (DUMAINE)

When we decided to move, my mom talked about moving to an apartment across the river so we could be closer to Tammi and Nakia. Over there, I would had to make friends with new people, so when I found out I was moving to Dumaine, I was kind of happy cause I was already familiar with the neighborhood.

On Dumaine Street I live in a six-plex apartment. In the wintertime, I won't have to wake up and go and stand by the heater in the morning because the house will already be warm. My mom says, "An apartment is not very hard to keep together and to decorate. They're more modern—very much more modern. And then the ceilings are low. See that burner on that stove over there? And it's very warm and very comfortable. Very comfortable." When I tell people where I live, they always ask, "Where at on Dumaine?" Because there are mostly houses on the street. They are different from the ones on North Dorgenois. They are more like the same and much closer together. One thing that is similar is that there's another church on my block.

The majority of the people on my block rent. It's a mixture of older and younger black people. The block has a lot of kids outside playing, riding their bikes, and making up a lot of noise. Sometimes it's nice to hear a little noise. Dumaine is more like a

neighborhood that has DJs and lots of parties. Your neighbors won't say, "Oh that's too loud, turn that down."

When my family had a party on Dorgenois, one of the two old men that used to stay in that big house where the Snyders live now got in the street and told us to lower the volume. Those two old men used to think they owned the block. But I had to give it to them; they kept their yard and sidewalk clean. Now that big, pretty house is up for sale again. Before the doctor bought it, it stayed up for sale a long, long time. I wonder who's going to buy it next.

All the youngsters in the neighborhood call Dumaine "D-Block." They call the intersection of Dorgenois and Dumaine, "D&D." On North Dorgenois where I used to live they didn't have a special name for it. People just called it how they saw it. If you like to live somewhere quiet, North Dorgenois between Barracks and Governor Nicholls would be perfect for you. Dumaine is for anyone who likes to sit outside and have fun.

THE NEIGHBORHOOD STORY PROJECT
OUR STORIES TOLD BY US

What you have just read is one of the five books to come from the first year of the Neighborhood Story Project. This has been an incredible year for us, and we thank you for your support and attention.

The Neighborhood Story Project would like to give a big shout out to the people of the City of New Orleans—y'all are the best. Thank you for showing so much love.

There are lots of folks and organizations that have made this possible. You have come through with stories, with food, with love, and with money—and believe us when we say that all four are necessary.

First off, we'd like to acknowledge our great partners, the Literacy Alliance of Greater New Orleans and the University of New Orleans. Specifically, Peg Reese, Rachel Nicolosi, Rick Barton, Tim Joder, Bob Cashner, Susan Krantz and Jeffrey Ehrenreich have been excellent supervisors and colleagues.

To Steve Gleason and Josselyn Miller at the One Sweet World Foundation. Thank-you for getting this project from the very beginning, and for having such awesome follow through.

To the institutions of the city that have been good to us—thank you. Good institutions play such an important role in making a place. Specifically we'd like to thank the Greater New Orleans Foundation, The Lupin Foundation, The Louisiana Endowment for the Humanities, Tulane Service Learning, The Schweser Family Foundation, and the guys from the Cultivating Community Program for donating the proceeds from your work with Longue Vue to help us get these books out.

To all of the individuals who have stepped up and given so much—from the donation of stamps to all the folks who have trusted us with their money. To Phyllis Sassoon and Mick Abraham for donating their cars. To all the folks who contributed, from the change jars at Whole Foods to the checks and food donations.

Thanks to our incredible steering committee, GK Darby, Peter Cook, Norbert Estrella, Tim Lupin, and Eliza Wells.

To Kalamu ya Salaam and Jim Randels at SAC, for taking us in and showing us the ropes, and giving us support as we try to grow. If we have done anything right as teachers it is because you have taught us.

To the administration of John McDonogh Senior High, Principal Spencer, and the past principals Winfield and Goodwin, thank you for being such great partners. To Ms. Pratcher and Ms. Tuckerson, thank you and bless you for dealing with all the headaches we cause. And to the staff at John McDonogh, we are so proud to be working with you.

To Elena Reeves and Kenneth Robin at the Tchopshop, thanks for being great designers, and for being such great sports about working with us. And to Jenny LeBlanc and Kyle Bravo at Hot Iron Press, thank you for being great designers/printer and for moving to town.

To Lauren Schug and Heather Booth, for transcribing and transcribing, above and beyond the call of duty.

To Anita Yesho for copy editing at short notice.

To Stephanie Oberhoff, and Communities in Schools- your mission is beautiful and your execution is great.

To Beverly McKenna, thank you for giving us such a beautiful office when we were only a sliver of an idea.

To Gareth Breunlin, who laid out the books and designed the covers. You have made our ideas come out on paper in a way that has honored all of the work and love involved.

To Davey and Jamie for being our dogs.

To Jerry for grant-writing, copy-editing, and being our hero.

To Dan, for his constant input, sharing a car and a computer, writing grants and cooking numerous dinners for the NSP.

To Shana, for promoting this project like it was your own, and for the input and help and grace.

And our biggest thank-you and respect to all of the Bolding, Jackson, Nelson, Price, and Wylie families. Without your love and care, this would not have been possible. Thank you for believing in the project and the work, and for making these books what they are.

And to Palmyra, Lafitte, St. Claude, Dorgenois (and the rest of Ebony's Sixth Ward), and N. Miro, thank you for your stories. We hope you like the books as much we liked making them.

The list is so long because so many of you have contributed.

Thanks for reading.

For the Neighborhood Story Project

Rachel Breunlin
Abram Himelstein

P.S. Thanks to Richard Nash, Ammi Emergency and Soft Skull Press for believing in us and New Orleans in our time of need.